Costume in Context

The 1920s and 1930s

Jennifer Ruby

B.T. Batsford Ltd, London

Foreword

When studying costume it is important to understand the difference between fashion and costume. Fashion tends to predict the future – that is, what people *will* be wearing – and very fashionable clothes are usually worn only by people wealthy enough to afford them. For example, even today, the clothes that appear in fashionable magazines are not the same as those being worn by the majority of people in the street. Costume, on the other hand, represents what people are actually wearing at a given time, which may be quite different from what is termed 'fashionable' for their day.

Each book in this series is built round a fictitious family. By following the various members, sometimes over several generations – and the people with whom they come into contact – you will be able to see the major fashion developments of the period and compare the clothing and lifestyles of people from all walks of life. You will meet servants, soldiers, street-sellers and beggars as well as the very wealthy, and you will see how their different clothing reflects their particular occupations and circumstances.

Major social changes are mentioned in each period and you will see how clothing is adapted as people's needs and attitudes change. The date list will help you to understand more fully how historical events affect the clothes that people wear.

Many of the drawings in these books have been taken from contemporary paintings or photographs. During the course of your work perhaps you could visit some museums and art galleries yourself in order to learn more about the costumes of the period you are studying from the artists who worked at that time.

c. 1932

This book is dedicated to the memory of my grandparents, whose courage gave me inspiration.

Acknowledgments

My thanks to Lillian Braithwaite, who shared her memories with me and love to my father who gave me the story.

Some of the illustrations have been taken from contemporary fashion plates and pictures. In particular:

Page 18, after a drawing by John Held Jr; page 34, after Anne Rochester.

Colour Plates: 'Evening Song' after George Barber, 'Hiking' after J.W. Tucker, the 'Dance Craze' after a *Punch* Cartoon and 'Gazette du Bon Ton', 'Yellow Car' after Weager.

© Jennifer Ruby 1988
First published 1988
Reprinted 1992

Typeset by Tek-Art Ltd, Kent
and printed and bound in Great Britain
by The Bath Press, Somerset
for the publishers
B.T. Batsford Ltd
4 Fitzhardinge Street
London W1H 0AH

ISBN 0 7134 5773 2

Contents

c. 1922

Date List

Early 1920s	The ideal female figure is a straight line, the natural waist is disguised and belts and sashes are worn around the hips. The brassière becomes a flattener – an essential part of the straight look. Lounge suits are popular for men. Throughout the period children's clothes are simple and practical.
1921	Artificial silk is on the market for the first time. It is known as Rayon from 1924. Elastic is being used more in corsetry.
1922	Beauty is becoming big business. The first ever articles on beauty appear. Forms of electrical massage are advertised.
1922	The BBC makes the first regular broadcasts on sound radio.
1923	Chanel makes suntanning fashionable.
1925	Oxford bags are popular, skirts are becoming shorter.
1926	The General Strike (3-12 May).
1927	BBC established by Royal Charter
1928	The first 'talkies' shown in British picture houses.
1929	The Wall Street Crash. The New York Stock Exchange collapses, setting off worldwide depression.
1930	Unemployment reaches 2½ million.
	Berlei (UK) is established and introduces a system of sizing for women's underwear.
1931	The Sunday Express calculates that 1500 lipsticks are being sold in London for every one sold previously.
1933-4	The zip fastener is being used more in the manufacture of clothes.
1935	The driving test is introduced.
1936	Edward VII abdicates to marry Mrs Wallis Simpson.
	The Jarrow March (October 5th).
	Shoulders become padded and square in women's clothes, giving them a slight military look.
1939	The Americans begin the production of nylon.
	The outbreak of World War II.

Introduction

Nineteen twenty to 1939 was a period which saw many changes in society, and these were reflected in fluctuating fashions. Communications improved. More people drove cars, flew in aeroplanes and travelled abroad. The BBC began broadcasting in the 1920s, cinema going became a popular passtime, and there were many more books, newspapers and magazines in circulation. Better communications meant that fashions travelled more quickly from cities to other areas and fashions from abroad were more quickly copied at home.

In the 1920s it was as if fashions were reflecting a sense of relief after World War One. There was a feeling of relaxation and a lifting of restrictions. Fashionable women abandoned their tight-fitting clothes, cut their hair, wore their skirts shorter, (though they did not become knee length until 1925/26), and danced the Charleston all night. As women moved towards emancipation, their clothes became less feminine and took on masculine attributes. A boyish look was admired and in order to achieve this, bosoms were flattened and waists disappeared. Tweed suits were often worn and the predominantly male pursuits of motoring and smoking were taken up by many young women.

The Wall Street Crash in 1929 brought an end to the euphoria and directly influenced fashion. Many people were made redundant when companies collapsed and there was less money available for the production or purchase of fancy clothes. With the Depression came more practical and less frivolous fashions. Skirts became longer, hair was grown and waists returned to their natural position. The look was a more feminine one, although a hint of masculinity remained with the fashion for wide-padded shoulders. Backs now became the centre of attention instead of legs and backless evening gowns were popular. Zip fastenings and greater use of elastic in the manufacture of clothes made garments easier to wear and the new method of bias cutting made them cling to the body. Make-up was worn more and more as women copied the looks of screen goddesses like Greta Garbo, Joan Crawford and Marlene Dietrich.

Sadly, men's clothes were rather unexciting during this period. The lounge suit remained popular for day wear, though it was usually worn in sombre colours. There was, however, a move towards greater freedom and a relaxing of convention in dress. Sports clothes were worn more often, and these added a dash of colour. The Prince of Wales, a favourite with all classes, did a great deal, by example, to popularize Fair Isle sweaters and knickerbockers, both garments which were worn for relaxing. One notable fashion of the period was the Oxford bags of 1925, which supposedly originated when Oxford undergraduate oarsmen wore baggy trousers over their shorts.

Children's clothes were much more practical than they had been in the

c. 1923

5

c. 1924

c. 1924

c. 1930

c. 1925

c. 1936

c. 1926

c. 1924

c. 1930

c. 1929

c. 1923

6

past. People were beginning to listen to the child psychologists who said that children needed freedom to explore, play and learn. Consequently, their clothes were less fussy and more sensible. Babies wore romper suits, little boys wore short trousers and loose shirts and little girls wore comfortable smock dresses. Two great influences on children's clothes were Royalty and Hollywood. Mothers everywhere dressed their little girls in clothes similar to those worn by the young Princesses Elizabeth and Margaret, and Shirley Temple, the child star of the 1930s, was a model for thousands of children with her curly hair and pretty dresses. In 1939, however, fashion and freedom evaporated as thousands of children were evacuated to the safety of the country, away from the bombing raids in the cities.

Another important change was the development of man-made fibres which contributed to the production of practical, inexpensive clothing. Rayon (artificial silk) was being used more and more and nylon appeared in the USA in 1938. Fashionable, washable dresses were mass produced and distributed through the growing network of department stores and 'Guinea Stores'. This meant that ordinary working women could now afford to be fashionable and this, in turn, helped to contribute towards a levelling of classes.

At the other end of the scale to the fashionable rich were the many unemployed who experienced very difficult times during the 1920s and 1930s. Scarcely able to scrape enough money together for food, they were obviously little concerned with fashion. Working men everywhere wore what seemed like a uniform consisting of a cloth cap, jacket, waistcoat and trousers and a neck scarf, and their wives did the best they could borrowing, mending, making or buying second hand clothes for themselves and their children. The General Strike in 1926 and Jarrow March in 1936 highlighted the plight of working people. Both events achieved very little, yet they were important as they demonstrated that working people were beginning to stand up and fight for themselves.

In this book you will meet people from all walks of life and you will see how their clothes reflect their lifestyles and circumstances. Think about some of the points mentioned above while you are reading so that you can not only learn about costume but also how it felt to live and work in the 1920s and 1930s.

A Wealthy Landowner, c. 1923

This is Colonel Richardson, a wealthy landowner who lives with his wife and family on a large country estate in the North of England. As he is a rich man, he can afford fashionable and expensive clothes for himself and his family.

In this picture he is wearing the correct clothes for formal daytime wear. He has on a three-piece lounge suit in herringbone which has a narrow fitting jacket and trousers with turn-ups. He is also wearing a striped shirt, a black tie and bowler hat, shoes and spats. He is carrying his raincoat and cane.

Edward, the Prince of Wales, was a great men's trend-setter at this time. He liked to play golf in baggy knickerbockers worn with Fair Isle sweaters, pattern socks and a flat tweed cap. Soon this outfit was adopted by golf players everywhere and similar clothes became very popular for informal day wear.

On the right you can see the Colonel relaxing. He is wearing a tweed cap, a knitted sweater, checked tweed knickerbockers, checked stockings and lace-up shoes. Also pictured on the opposite page are one of his sports jackets and two different styles of shoe.

golf outfit

sports jacket

patent leather walking shoe

patent day-dress shoe or boot with cloth top

The Landowner's Wife, c. 1923

This is the Colonel's wife, Cecily, who is wearing the latest in fashionable clothes.

After the emancipation and freedom that women had achieved for themselves during World War I, there was, in the early 1920s, a noticeable change in styles of dress. As women now considered themselves to be equal to men, it was no longer fashionable to emphasize their femininity. Instead, a boyish, masculine look was sought, confirming the new found freedom and independence. Ladies cut their hair short, flattened their breasts and disguised their waists in order to achieve the 'ideal' figure, which was a straight line!

Cecily is wearing an afternoon frock of silk and wool morocain. The dress is unshaped and the waistline is dropped to the level of the hips. Her hat is in the cloche style and is also made of morocain. She is wearing high-heeled court shoes with decorative buckles, coloured beads and pendant earings, which were fashionable with short hair.

The popularity of domestic knitting during the war resulted in knitted jumpers becoming fashionable. They were usually worn with a matching or contrasting skirt for informal wear. On the right you can see some other items from Cecily's wardrobe, including a knitted jumper and a silk blouse.

As always, women are disguising and altering their true shapes for fashion and you can see that Cecily achieves her flat chested straight figure by wearing a flattener bra and corset. Most women now wear their hair short, either in a bob or shingled. Cecily's maid curls her hair for her with curling tongs.

cloche hat —
wool-embroidered
straw

black cloche hat with
ribbon trimming

cross-over jumper

silk blouse, coloured
stripes

handbags

flat-look lace brassière

woven corset and
"flattener" bra

shoes

curling tongs

Their Children, c. 1924

During the early 1920s, people began to take a new look at their children. They listened to the child psychologists who said that children should be given more freedom to play, explore and learn. So now, instead of being punished if they got their clothes dirty, children were allowed to get messy while they played games and enjoyed themselves. These new attitudes meant that frills, ruffles and lace were now seen as impractical for children's wear and more comfortable outfits were adopted. Very young children wore one-piece romper suits, little boys wore short trousers, loose shirts and jackets, and little girls wore comfortable smock dresses.

Here are Elizabeth, Edward and Emmeline, the Colonel's three children. Elizabeth is eight years old. She is wearing a loose-fitting cotton dress with a dropped waist and half sleeves, white cotton socks and practical shoes.

Her brother Edward goes to an expensive boarding school. Here you can see him wearing his school uniform, which consists of a cap, a blazer, flannel trousers and his school tie.

Emmeline is a young lady of 17, so she loves to wear the latest fashions. Here she has on a cloche hat, a woollen jacket, a pleated skirt and a loose jumper with a low neck, around which she has draped a decorative scarf. Detachable collars, cuffs and jabots were very popular at this time as they meant that a lady could achieve a different look with the same blouse by varying her accessories. Below are some from Emmeline's wardrobe. You can also see some of her other accessories.

linen handker-
chief with
hand embroidery

shoes

muslin collar and cuffs

embroidered
modesty
front

fine muslin collar
and cuffs

net jabot, trimmed with lace

Domestic Servants, c. 1925

On the left are three of the Colonel's servants, Blanche, Libby and Susan. They are all housemaids and are wearing black dresses, white caps and aprons. The girls live in at the Colonel's house and have a varied range of duties such as making the fires in the morning, dusting and cleaning, and serving tea in the afternoon.

Emmeline sometimes surpervises the maids if she wants something arranged specially. For example, occasionally, she might be having friends around for cocktails, so she would then ensure that the maids have everything arranged perfectly for her guests. Here, Emmeline is wearing an overall wrap to protect her clothes while she is organizing things for an evening gathering. In this picture you can see her shingled hair more clearly. It is a very severe hairstyle compared to the elaborate *coiffures* favoured in Edwardian times.

Fashion, c. 1925

This is Charles, Emmeline's fiancé, who is training to be a doctor. He comes from a wealthy family and has plenty of money to spend on clothes and leisure pursuits. In this picture he is wearing a light blue woollen jacket and waistcoat and grey flannel trousers. His trousers are very wide in the leg and are called Oxford bags. This style is very popular with young men and sometimes the width of their trousers is as much as 32 inches! Charles is taking Emmeline out to lunch in his new car.

Emmeline is wearing a red fox fur – still complete with its head and tail – and a tailored suit consisting of a light wool jacket and checked skirt. A bow tie, cane and cloche hat complete her outfit. Like many women at this time, Emmeline is wearing clothes that give her a rather mannish appearance. This emphasizes her independence. She wants to be seen as a capable and independent young woman, not as a helpless female dressed in frills and lace.

Short skirts (knee length) were becoming more and more popular at this time and many people were shocked at the new fashions. Clergymen around the world declared that they were the work of the Devil and the Archbishop of Naples claimed that a recent earthquake was due to God's anger at the indecent exposure!

As legs were on show more than ever before, women began to spend more money on their stockings, as these were no longer hidden by yards of material. Many of these stockings were made of silk and were very expensive. Sometimes they had decorations down the side or at the heel. It is interesting that approximately 60 years on from this date, The Princess of Wales would be influential in bringing this fashion back.

pure silk and lisle stockings

The Bright Young Things, c. 1926

Charles and Emmeline have a very active social life. They go out motoring, bathing and picknicking, they play tennis and golf and dance away the nights with their friends. Here you can see them doing the Charleston, an energetic and popular dance of the 1920s.

Emmeline is wearing a sleeveless straight-line sheath dress with a slightly irregular hem line made of lilac-coloured tulle and sewn with sequins of several shade of mauve. Her silk stockings are rolled and gartered and her shoes have Louis heels — which means that they are curved at the front. Her jangling bangles, swinging beads and shingled hair complete the carefree boyish look so popular in the 1920s. Charles is wearing an evening suit with a white waistcoat and bow tie and patent leather shoes.

In 1923, the famous designer, Coco Chanel, returned from a cruise with a sun tan and suddenly sunbathing became fashionable. Trips abroad and days at the seaside became more popular as men and women strove to acquire the bronzed and healthy look that we still admire today. (It is interesting that Coco Chanel started the fashion for sunbathing in the 1920s and today, in the 1980s, her company has been the first to introduce colour cosmetics with a built-in protection against the damage caused by the sun's harmful rays!)

On the right, Emmeline is enjoying a day on the beach. She is wearing a bathing suit of two shades of orange jersey, silk beach shoes and a rubber hat.

Charles is dressed in clothes that he might wear to go punting or picnicking in. He has on a light coloured flannel jacket, blue-grey flannel trousers with lapped side seams, and a panama hat.

When he is playing tennis he wears cream or white flannel trousers and shirt, a belt, scarf or tie around his waist, white canvas boots, a white sweater and a navy blue blazer or cap.

In the 1920s young people who led very hectic social lives were known as the 'Bright Young Things'. Find out more about some of their activities and draw pictures of some of their outfits, particularly the 'flappers'.

A Schoolmistress and her pupils, c. 1926

Over the next few pages you will meet some other people who live and work not far from the Colonel's estate.

This is Lydia, the schoolmistress at the local village school.

Lydia is wearing a more practical form of dress favoured by working women. She has on a deep-crowned hat with a brim, a long, loose, belted jacket over a white blouse and a full, long skirt. This style of skirt had been fashionable for informal wear ten years earlier but it continued to be worn by many women in the 1920s, as it was so easy and comfortable for working in. The fact that Lydia is cycling alone in the countryside without an escort reflects the new freedom that women can now enjoy since the war.

These children are three of Lydia's pupils at the school. Their parents do not have much money so their clothes are often very worn and ill fitting, as they have usually been passed down from an older brother or sister.

Len and Jack are brothers and their father is a farm worker. Both boys are wearing knitted jumpers, short trousers and lace-up shoes and Jack has an old school cap on his head. Beth's father is a gardener on the Colonel's estate. She attends Lydia's school with her younger sister. Beth is wearing a white blouse, a knitted cardigan which is too small for her, a navy gym tunic, woollen socks and bar shoes.

A Shopkeeper and his Wife, c. 1926

This is Lillian. She and her husband William run a baker's and confectioner's shop in a large town a few miles away.

Lillian is wearing a striped cotton dress with a dropped waist, large white collar with lace edging, and a navy tie. Her hair is in a bob with a decorative slide at the side. She also has on gold rimmed spectacles which cost her a great deal of money. When she is serving in the shop Lillian wears a heavy cotton overall over her clothes.

On the right you can see her and William behind the counter. William is wearing a dark blue lounge suit, a white cotton shirt and a navy tie.

The couple sell bread, flour, cakes, tinned fruit and sweets that they make themselves. They also make their own ice cream. Recently they bought an American soda fountain and had it installed in the shop. This new idea is very popular with their customers who come and sit at the little tables in the shop and enjoy an ice-cream soda.

Look at some of the items for sale in Lillian and William's shop. Can you see any brand names that you recognize that are still available today? Look at the scales that William uses. Can you see the weights for measuring up quantities? Try and think of all the differences between a shop like this and the supermarkets that we have today. Which do you prefer? Draw a picture of William and Lillian in their kitchen making sweets. What would they be wearing?

A Labourer and his Family, c. 1926

This is John, who lives with his family in the same town as Lillian and William. He used to be a miner but he had to give up his job because the work involved long periods of standing waist high in water, which gave him a severe skin rash. Now he works as a labourer in the shipyards. He is wearing a waistcoat and unmatching trousers, a striped cotton shirt and boots. Like many working men, John does not wear a collar or tie. When he is working, he usually wears a scarf around his neck to absorb perspiration in the summer and keep him warm in the winter.

John lives with his wife Sarah and their new baby Joe in a tenement building occupied by several families. John and Sarah live in two rooms. In the backyard there is one toilet, (known as the 'netty'), and one tap which everyone must share.

Sarah is wearing a knitted short-sleeved jumper over a long-sleeved cotton blouse, a checked cotton apron and a woollen skirt. She is holding Baby Joe, wrapped up in a blanket.

Under the chest of drawers on the left are John's new boots. He is very proud of these as he obtained them by collecting tokens from the packets of 'Club' cigarettes that he smokes. He never wears them but keeps them to show visitors.

John and Sarah live in very cramped and difficult conditions. What do you think it would have been like to share one toilet and one tap with several other families? How difficult would this have been for Sarah and her new baby?

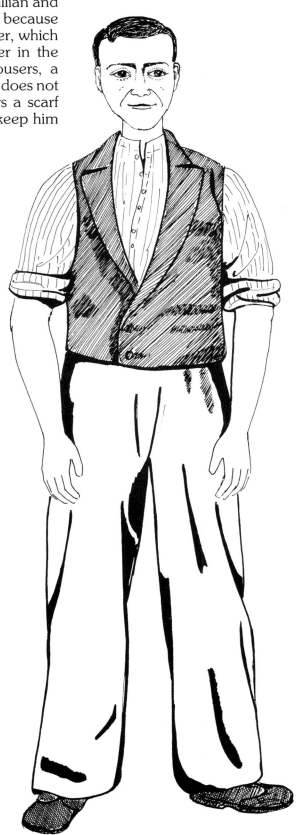

Miners, 1926

This is Bill, one of John's friends from the mines. He is wearing a flat cap, a coarse linen shirt, a woollen waistcoat and trousers which are hitched up at the knee by two leather straps. He is also wearing a scarf around his neck and stout boots. The leather straps across his chest are for securing a pad on his back which protects him when he is 'righting' waggons that have come of the tracks in the mine.

Another miner, Albert is working deep in the mine with his pickaxe. It is very hot and heavy work, so he has removed his shirt and is wearing only his trousers and boots, which have steel segments attached to the soles in order to stop the soles wearing out too quickly.

Albert's Davy lamp is by his side. Find out why this lamp was such an important invention for the miners.

In the 1920s the miners worked in very difficult and dangerous conditions for very low wages. In 1926 they came out on strike. Thousands of other workers supported them and eventually the whole country was brought to a standstill in the famous 'General Strike', which lasted for nine days. Find out all you can about the General Strike. Who was involved? Who were the Strike Breakers? What did the Government do?

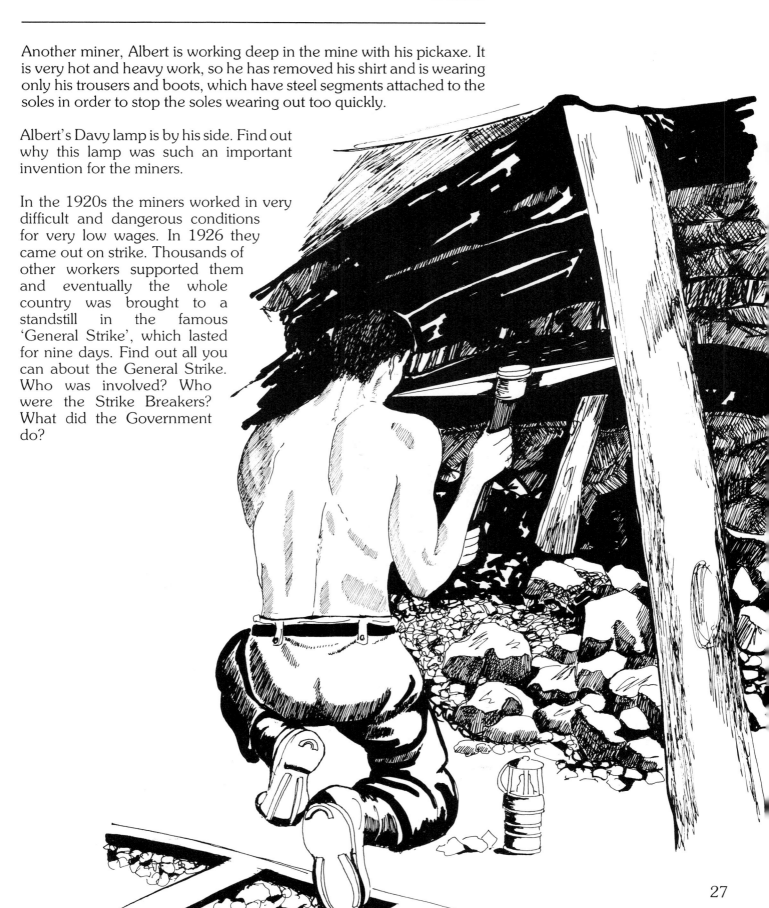

A Wedding, c. 1927

We will now return to the Colonel's family home, where there is great excitement because it is Emmeline's wedding day. Here you can see her in her bedroom with two of her friends, Audrey and Gloria, who are to be her bridesmaids. They have stayed the night and are now in Emmeline's room talking excitedly about what they are going to wear.

Emmeline (seated) and Audrey are both wearing long satin nightdresses and slippers. Gloria is wearing her cami-knickers and has her matching nightdress over her arm. All three girls have on boudoir caps which they wear at night to protect their hair. The fashion in nightwear and underwear is, as for day wear, to keep the figure as slim and boyish looking as possible.

Emmeline's cosmetics are on the table behind her. See if you can find out more about the fashion in make-up in the 1920s.

In this picture you can see Emmeline's wedding dress. It is made of ivory georgette and is embroidered with silver and crystal beads. Her headdress is also made from silver beads which have been arranged in flower shapes. Emmeline has grown her hair a little longer for the wedding and has it styled in soft curls. Underneath her dress Emmeline is wearing lace-trimmed cami-knickers and also a dress shield like the one pictured below, which is designed to prevent perspiration spoiling her dress.

cami-knickers
in georgette

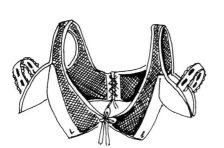

dress shield

A Bridegroom and Wedding Guests, c. 1927

Here is Charles in his wedding outfit. He is wearing a single-breasted morning coat with braided edges, a matching single-breasted waistcoat, a silk top hat and striped trousers. His shirt has a wing collar and he has white gloves and spats.

On the right you can see some of the wedding guests. Many of the ladies at the wedding are wearing light dresses made of printed chiffons, silks and organdies, like those pictured here. Large brimmed hats and high-heeled shoes are also popular.

The fashion for short skirts in the mid 1920s did not please everyone. It was true that silk stocking manufacturers were enjoying a boom in trade but the skimpy dresses did not bring much profit to cloth manufacturers. So for some time designers endeavoured to lower hemlines and the first experiments, aimed at persuading women to adopt longer skirts, included designs where the back of the skirt was longer than the front, or a long panel was added at the side or the back. Examples of these are shown on the right. These styles proved to be quite popular, but hemlines did not finally come down again until the end of the decade.

Henry, Charles's best man, has on a similar outfit to the bridegroom, except that he is wearing a matching grey waistcoat and trousers.

Find out more about the fashions of 1927 and draw a picture of some of the other wedding guests. Include some of the servants who might be helping out at the wedding feast. What would have been on the menu?

Designer Clothes – Chanel, c. 1927

On her honeymoon, Emmeline might have worn clothes by the famous designer, Gabrielle (Coco) Chanel. The appeal of Chanel's designs lay in their simplicity and classical lines. Her clothes were faultlessly elegant and chic. She made simple jersey suits and dresses very popular and also launched the fashion for costume jewellery. Chanel claimed that five was her lucky number and so she created Chanel Number 5 perfume, which is still worn by thousands of women today. Find out more about Coco Chanel and how she rose from humble beginnings to become world famous.

costume jewellery

tiered dress in black crêpe

striped jersey suit with matching hat and scarf

The Dance Craze, c. 1922

Evening song, c. 1923

Croquet players, c. 1926

On the telephone, c. 1927

The Ferryman, c. 1930

Yellow Car, c. 1933

Fashions, c. 1935

Hiking, c. 1936

Designer Clothes – Schiaparelli, c. 1930

Italian-born Elsa Schiaparelli was another designer of the period. A rival of Chanel, she was famous in the 1930s for her sportswear, unusual knitwear and outrageous backless dresses, which caused a sensation. Embroidery, unusual motifs and ornamental buttons made her designs exciting and they were worn by the rich and famous.

Like Chanel, Schiaparelli launched her own perfume. It was called 'Shocking' and was packaged in a bottle resembling the female torso! Schiaparelli's intention was always to cause a sensation and her originality and flair made her a fortune. Find out more about her and other famous designers like Mainbocher and Vionnet.

one of the famous knitted sweaters

black and white tweed

golfing outfit

A Housewife, c. 1930

This is Dorothy, Lydia's sister, who lives with her husband and children on the outskirts of the town. She used to be a schoolteacher like Lydia, but gave up her job when her children came along and now she stays at home caring for her family.

sleeveless
coatette
embroidered
and with
a monogram

Dorothy likes to sew and is often busy with a needle and thread. Here she is darning some of her husband's jumpers. She is wearing a matching jumper and skirt in green jersey and high-heeled shoes.

Sometimes she embroiders her clothes so that garments from a previous season can be given a new lease of life. On this page you can see two sleeveless coatettes and a scarf set that she has embroidered.

A magazine in 1930 suggested that most women needed 'attractive aprons for serving meals in' and that an apron could make 'a colourful and becoming addition to one's appearance'. One of Dorothy's aprons is pictured below. She made it herself from a magazine pattern.

Other magazines also emphasized the need to look beautiful at all times for one's husband, and that it was a woman's *duty* never to neglect her appearance. One magazine advised: '*Never* let your husband *see* you in a grubby apron, a bedraggled dressing gown or a shabby working frock — many a happy marriage has been wrecked because some foolish wife kept her prettiest garments for visitors and wore "any old thing" about the house.'*

Lydia is a feminist and is often telling Dorothy that her young sons ought to be taught how to do their own mending and to help with the housework because Dorothy would like to go back to work. This is a new idea and Dorothy is not sure about giving 'women's work' to her sons. Lydia argues that it would be foolish for a professional woman to try and do everything. What do you think? How do the above attitudes compare with those of today?

brown
velveteen
coatette
with gold
embroidery

jade green cap, scarf and gloves, embroidered with orange

serving apron

*Quote from Woman's Own,
October 15, 1932

A Bank Clerk and his Children, c. 1930

Here are Dorothy's husband, Harry, and their two children, Richard and Anthony. Harry works in a bank so he often wears a smart suit like the one pictured here, which is double breasted and is made of dark blue serge. He is also wearing a snap brim hat, which means that the brim can be turned down at the front and up at the back in the fashionable manner. A white cotton shirt, a striped tie and lace up shoes complete his outfit and he carries a cane.

Richard is eight years old. He is wearing a double-breasted jacket and trousers made of grey flannel, grey knitted socks and lace-up shoes. His little brother Anthony is wearing a romper suit knitted by Dorothy, short white socks and soft leather shoes.

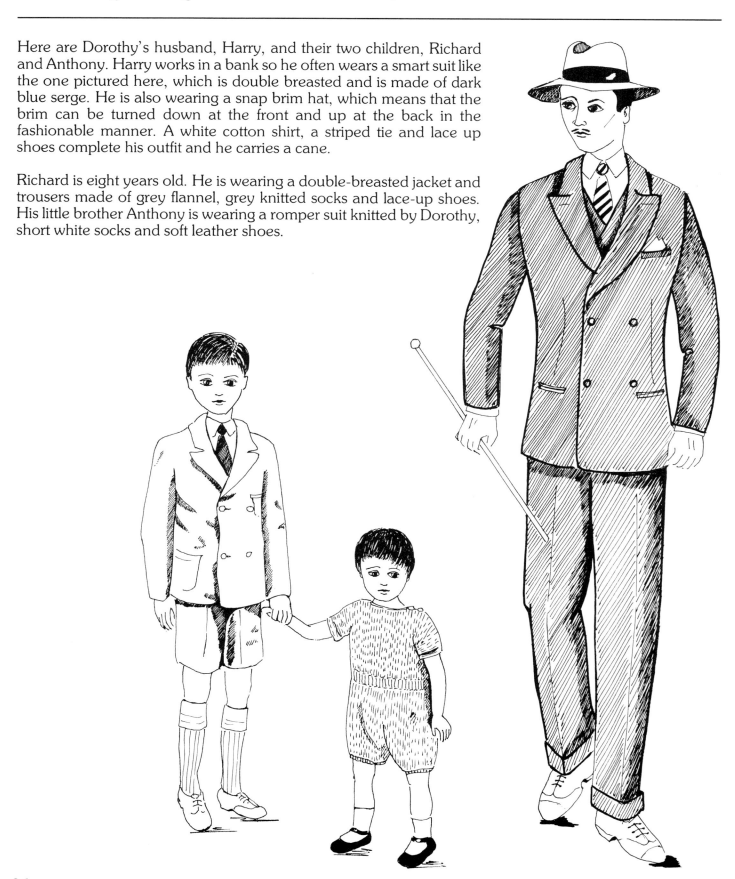

An Unemployed Man and his Children, c. 1930

In a street not far away we meet Tom, who is an unemployed labourer. He used to work in the shipyards but was made redundant four years ago. He is very sad and depressed because he has been out of work for so long and he spends many hours wandering the streets looking for odd jobs. Sometimes he goes to the local pub to drown his depression in drink. He is wearing a soft cap, a striped jacket and waistcoat and a woollen scarf around his neck. His heavy cotton trousers have been patched and on his feet he is wearing clogs, which have thick leather uppers and wooden soles.

His children, Alice and George, have come to find him and take him home for dinner. Alice is wearing a knitted cardigan over her white blouse and gym tunic, which is tied in the middle with a piece of string. George is wearing an old knitted jumper over short trousers, woollen socks and leather shoes.

Compare these two fathers and their children. How are their lives different? Think about how Tom's wife might look. Draw a picture of her. Try to picture accurately the type of clothes she would wear.

Making Ends Meet, c. 1932

We will now return to John and Sarah. John has been unemployed for six years. He, like Tom, was made redundant from the shipyards. Things have been very difficult during this time and, in order to save money on fuel, John often goes to the beach and collects coal that that has been washed up by the tide. The salt from the sea water makes it glow brightly in the fire when it is burning.

Here you can see him returning from the beach, balancing his sack of coal on his bicycle. He is wearing a soft, flat cap, a scarf around his neck, unmatching jacket and trousers, and heavy boots. His trouser legs are secured around the ankles with string to keep them out of the way when cycling.

Sarah is able to draw £1 per week from the government on which to keep the family. Out of this she gives John 2/6 (12½p) for his pocket money. Obviously what is left is not enough for her to manage on. Here you can see her outside a pawn shop where she has just pawned John's prize boots without him knowing.

She is wearing a woollen shawl over a cotton blouse and skirt, woollen stockings and heeled shoes. Joe is wearing a cotton shirt, short trousers with braces, woollen socks and lace-up shoes.

Sarah likes to read but her eyes are a little weak. Her glasses come from Woolworths and cost sixpence. Her eyes have never been tested; instead Sarah just tried on various pairs and decided that she could see 'really smashing' with a pair of number 20s, which she bought. What kind of problems might arise from such a haphazard method of choosing and buying spectacles?

Sarah also earns a little extra money by telling fortunes for women who go to her house. Sarah reads their tea cups while Joe stands at the door watching for the local policeman, as fortune telling is against the law.

What do you think it would be like to live like this? How does this compare with being on the dole today?

Women's Fashions, c. 1933

Now we will return to Emmeline, who is living with Charles and their two young children in London. Fashions have changed somewhat since you last saw her. Waistlines have risen, skirt lengths have fallen, hair is longer and heels are higher. Altogether, the look is much more feminine than the boyish figure of the 1920s.

On the right Emmeline is wearing a brightly coloured floral print dress with a black ribbon sash and trimmings. Her hat has a medium brim and ribbon trim and she is wearing high heeled court shoes with decorative bows. She is carrying her bag.

The fashionable silhouette is long and slim and many women, like Emmeline, wear a corselette in order to achieve the right shape. During the 1930s there were great advances in corsetry. Berlei (UK) was established in 1930 and it brought a system of sizing to Britain. This meant that a woman's figure type was now taken into account and she could be properly fitted and measured for her corset by a trained saleswoman. Elastic was being used more and more in corsets, making them much more comfortable, and in 1933 the zip fastener appeared, which eliminated all those hooks and eyes!

Make up was becoming more popular than in the 1920s with lips and nails becoming redder and redder. One newspaper of the time reported that kissing had gone out of fashion because of the high cost of cosmetics! Emmeline carries a powder compact in her bag and frequently buys creams from the new Elizabeth Arden range of beauty products.

Straight hair is not thought attractive and magazines are filled with advertisements for curling tongs and false pieces, though no woman would admit to wearing one of these!

On the right you can see some more garments from Emmeline's wardrobe. Find out more about what she might have worn and draw a picture of a suit and coat that she might have owned.

40

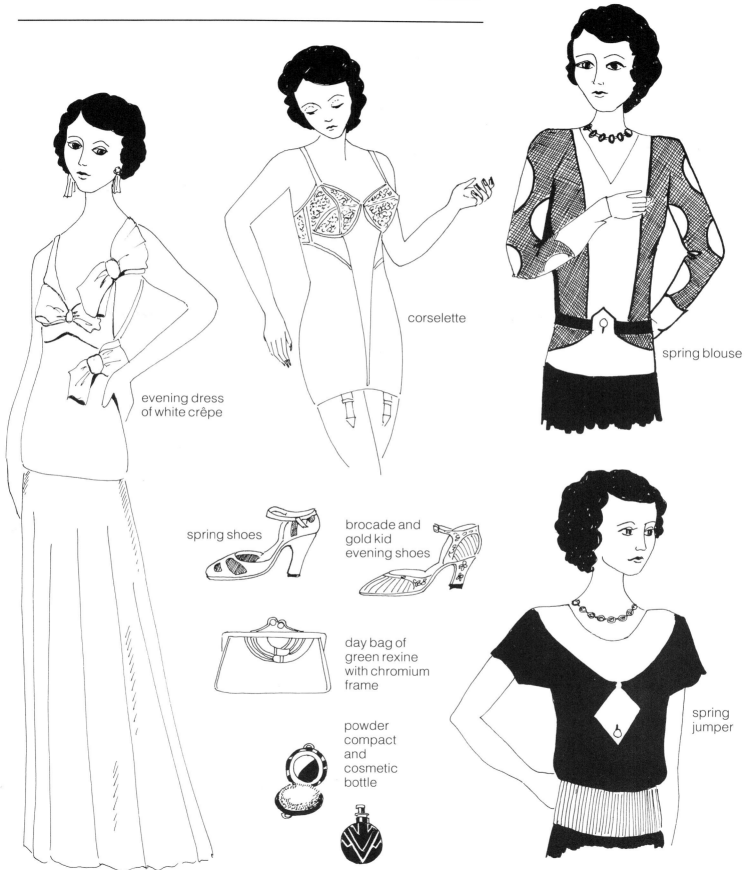

evening dress
of white crêpe

corselette

spring blouse

spring shoes

brocade and
gold kid
evening shoes

day bag of
green rexine
with chromium
frame

powder
compact
and
cosmetic
bottle

spring
jumper

Men's Clothes, c. 1933

The fashion in men's clothes changed very little during the 1920s and 1930s, the lounge suit continuing to be the most popular ordinary wear. Generally, clothes were rather dull, although they were relieved occasionally by sports clothes of more unconventional design or brightly coloured ties and socks.

Here is Charles, who is doing very well in his career as a doctor and now has a successful practice in Harley Street. He is wealthy and can afford smart fashionable clothes. In this picture he is wearing a belted mackintosh over his suit, although sometimes he might choose to wear a woollen overcoat like the one pictured opposite. The fashion in coats is for a long, lean look like that favoured by women. When at work he usually wears a lounge suit which might be made from serge or tweed and could be dark grey, brown, dark blue or black pin stripe. When Charles is relaxing at home he likes to wear knitted pullovers like the one in the picture. His hair is always short and he keeps it in place with hair cream.

Other items from his wardrobe are shown opposite. Charles also has many accessories. These include leather gloves, silk handkerchiefs, knitted silk and woollen scarves, umbrellas, and walking sticks. He also owns silver cigarette cases, jewelled cuff links and tie pins.

Some of Charles's patients are very wealthy. Imagine a rich man and woman who go to his surgery for a consultation. Draw them in the clothes that they might wear.

c. 1933

knitted
pullover

single-breasted
lounge suit
with wide
lapels

suspender belt
worn around
the calf to
hold up the
sock

two-tone
leather shoes
for leisure
wear

hand-sewn shoe
in box calf

double-
breasted
evening
waistcoat

single-
breasted
evening
waistcoat

In the Kitchen, c. 1933

Emmeline's sister Elizabeth and her fiancé Robert are coming to stay with Emmeline for the weekend. It is now quite fashionable for the lady of the house to dabble a little in the cooking preparations or make her own cocktails for her guests. Here you can see Emmeline in the kitchen with her cook, Daisy. Both women are wearing white cotton aprons over their dresses. Daisy's dress is, of course, quite simple compared with Emmeline's frilly one.

Daisy rather resents Madam's intrusion into her kitchen and would rather be left to get on with the cooking herself.

What is going to be on the menu?

Find out what some of the other servants would be wearing and draw pictures of them.

A Country Walk, c. 1933

It is Sunday and Emmeline and Elizabeth have driven into the country for a walk. Emmeline is wearing a fitted wine-coloured woollen suit. The jacket has a wide collar and the skirt has a centre back fastening. She also wears a 'Byron' bow at her neck, a knitted jumper and a round hat.

Elizabeth is wearing a fitted tweed suit in brown and beige. The jacket is belted and has four deep pockets. The skirt has inverted pleats at the front and back to allow room for walking. Both women wear comfortable walking shoes and carry canes.

Children's Clothes, c. 1934

During the 1930s children's clothes became even more practical and comfortable to wear. Corduroys, traditionally worn by British working men and farm labourers, became popular with boys, and little girls were seen in pleated skirts and woollen jerseys or soft, simple dresses. The royal family set some of these new trends and many women dressed their daughters in clothes copied from the young princesses Elizabeth and Margaret, and their babies in smocks like those worn by the Duke of Kent (b. 1935).

The worldwide fame of Shirley Temple, the child film star, also influenced children's fashions, and mothers everywhere modelled their children on Shirley and her clothes. In 1934 she starred in the film *Stand up and Sing*, in which she wore a red-and-white polka dot dress. This instantly became a mass fashion and was copied around the world. Find out more about Shirley Temple and her influence on children's fashions.

Here are Charles and Emmeline's three children, Oliver, James and Harriet. The boys are wearing soft cotton shirts, striped ties, short trousers, woollen socks and lace-up shoes. Harriet has on a simple smock dress and short socks. Her curly hair is modelled on Shirley Temple's. Harriet's hair is naturally straight, so her nurse uses a new product on it called 'Curly Top' to make it fashionably curly! On the opposite page you can see more examples of children's clothes from the 1930s.

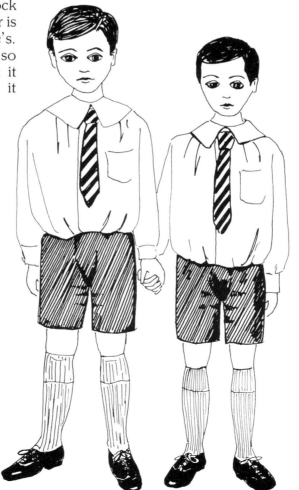

smock dress

woollen coats and hats

jersey and short trousers

knitted jersey and pleated skirt

leggings

romper suit

viyella blouse, short, buttoned trousers

woollen coat and cap

47

Looking for Work, c. 1934

Now, in contrast to Emmeline and her family, we will return to John and Sarah. John has been unemployed for eight years and things have been extremely difficult for him. He has now decided to try and find work further south. His plan is to start cycling south and to keep going until he finds a job, at which time he will send for Sarah and Joe to join him. He is wearing a cloth cap, a checked scarf around his neck, a shabby overcoat over his jacket and trousers and heavy boots. He has a packet of sandwiches and 2/6 in his pocket.

In fact, John cycled 250 miles before he found work as a ditch digger in a new town 20 miles north of London. His journey took him three days. Try to imagine what it would have been like. Travel was not as easy in the 1930s as it is today and for someone like John this would have been a tremendous adventure, taking enormous courage. He had to sleep under haystacks and ask for food and, as he travelled further south, some people found it hard to understand his north country accent. It must have felt like being in a foreign country. When John had secured his job, the government paid for Sarah and Joe to join him.

Over the next few pages you will see some of the people that he met on his journey.

Factory Workers, c. 1934

These three men all work in a car factory. They know John and have come out during their lunch break to wish him luck on his journey. The man on the right is wearing protective overalls made of heavy cotton and underneath these he has on a knitted jersey, a waistcoat and trousers. He has a scarf at his neck. The other two men do not have overalls and are working in their ordinary day clothes. All three are wearing cloth caps.

These men are employed to rub down the car bodies ready for painting. The job creates a great deal of dust and they do not have face masks, though they try and keep the dust down with water. The work is very hard, the hours are long and the rules are strict. For example, a man's pay is docked if he visits the toilet too often. However, all three are grateful to have work, however hard, in times of such high unemployment.

A Hot Potato Man, c. 1934

As John rides through the streets of the town he passes Bert, the hot potato man. Bert has a mobile boiler which he wheels around the streets and from it he sells scalding hot boiled potatoes which are liberally sprinkled with salt.

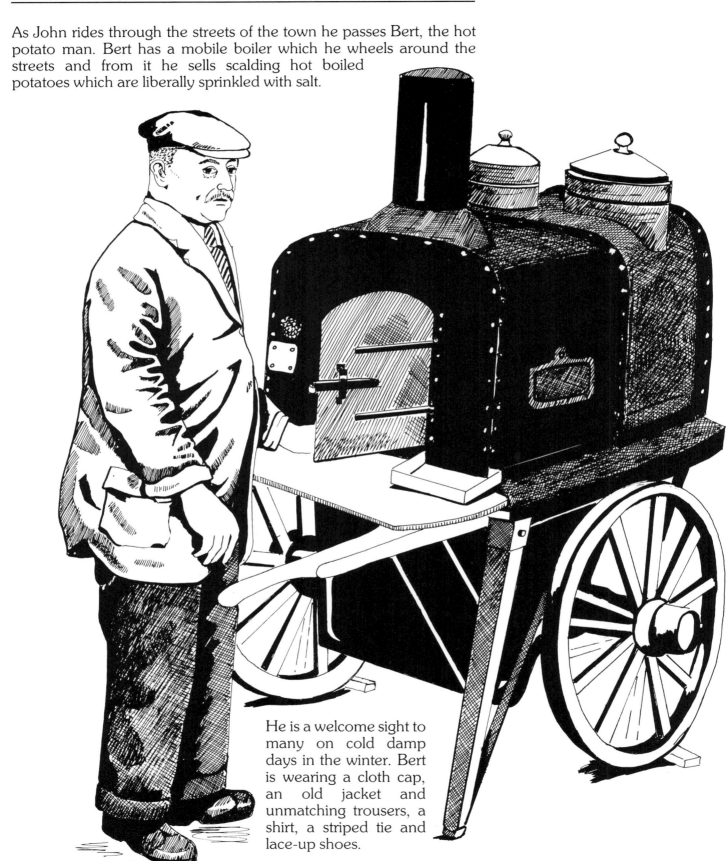

He is a welcome sight to many on cold damp days in the winter. Bert is wearing a cloth cap, an old jacket and unmatching trousers, a shirt, a striped tie and lace-up shoes.

Cleaning Fish, c. 1934

Bert's wife Hannah is a few streets away. She buys fish from the local port and sells it to the housewives round about. Here you can see her cleaning and cutting fish – to the delight of the local stray cats!

She is wearing a knitted waistcoat over a cotton blouse, a long woollen skirt, woollen socks, and carpet slippers instead of shoes, because her feet swell from standing all day. Her hair is tied back in a rather messy bun.

Bert and Hannah have made a living selling on the streets for many years. Find out more about street sellers in the 1920s and 1930s. What sort of clothes did they wear? Did any of them wear uniforms?

A Farm Worker and his Family, c. 1934

During the course of his three-day journey, John rode through towns and villages. Sometimes he met and chatted to country people like Albert and his family.

Albert (on the right) works as a farm hand and his eldest son Len, (whom you saw at the village school earlier in the book), works with him. Both men are wearing jackets, waistcoats and trousers, heavy boots and scarves around their necks. Albert has his trousers secured at the ankles with string to keep them out of the way while he is working and to stop mice running up his legs! Len is wearing a cloth cap and Albert an old trilby hat. They are busy sewing seeds. They walk up and down, scattering the seeds over the ground from their aprons which are made of sacking.

To us, this seems a very old fashioned way to sew seed. What methods do farmers use today?

c. 1934

Albert's wife Lizzie is standing outside their cottage with one of her daughters, Betty. Lizzie is dressed smartly but her clothes are rather old fashioned. This is both because she lives in the country and fashions take a while to reach country areas, and also because she does not have much money, so she keeps her dresses for several years.

She is wearing a black hat with a wide brim, a checked woollen, long-sleeved dress with a dropped waistline, and bar shoes. Betty is wearing a hand-knitted dress and hat, white socks and black shoes. In approximately which year would Lizzie's dress have been fashionable?

Although Albert and his family are quite poor, they do not go short of good food as they obtain fresh eggs, vegetables and salads from the farm and their small garden.

Compare the lives of Albert and Lizzie with John and Sarah. What advantages were there to living in the country?

A Landlady and her Daughter, c. 1934

When John finally found a job after cycling 250 miles south he also had to find somewhere to stay. This was not easy, as many landladies did not want to risk taking a lodger who was dishevelled and dirty, had no money and could not pay any rent until he had received his first week's wages. Eventually he found a lady willing to trust him. Her name was Maud, a widow who lived with her daughter.

Here you can see Maud doing her housework. She is wearing a printed cotton wraparound overall to protect her jumper and skirt while she is working. She is also wearing stockings and lace-up shoes. Her hair is very curly as her daughter, who is a hairdresser, has used a new 'permanent' method of curling it.

Maud is using a vacuum cleaner, which is a new labour saving device. Many homes now have electricity and housewives are finding their chores considerably easier with the aid of electric washing machines, polishers and heaters. There are also new gas cookers and boilers which make cooking easier and provide a good supply of hot water. Find out more about home improvements in the 1930s.

This is Irene, Maud's daughter. She loves going to the cinema each week and copying the make-up and hairstyles of the Hollywood filmstars like Greta Garbo and Joan Crawford. She also loves to buy and make clothes. There are many more ready-to-wear dresses available in the shops now. Shops like Marks and Spencer are selling women's fashions in their multiple stores and the growth of the rayon industry has meant that working girls like Irene can afford elegant, attractive and washable dresses which are being mass produced. At the Guinea Gown shops it is possible to buy a dress for exactly a guinea (21 shillings), so girls can afford 'dressy' outfits for dancing and cinema going.

Here Irene is wearing a printed cotton dress in a floral design. The two smaller pictures show dresses that she has made herself, after sending for the patterns from a woman's magazine.

Find out more about mass produced clothes in the 1920s and 1930s.

printed rayon dress
with frilled cowl collar

printed cotton dress
with wrap-over bodice

The Jarrow Crusade, 1936

In 1936, the unemployment in the north east of England was so bad that many people got together and decided to take action. On October 5 207 unemployed men from Jarrow began marching to London with a petition for the government signed by 11,572 people. The marchers called themselves the Jarrow Crusade. They were widely supported and large numbers of people turned out to watch them along the way.

Some of the men have stopped in a field for a meal. All of them are wearing cloth caps, jackets, waistcoats and trousers. They also have waterproof capes for the rain and the cook has on a white cotton jacket over his ordinary clothes. What do you think they are going to eat?

Parliament turned down the petition for help and the marchers returned home. How do you think they felt?

Robert and Elizabeth are now married and are living in London, where Robert is a successful barrister. Although they are unaffected by the hardships experienced by the unemployed, they nevertheless feel a great deal of sympathy for them and they have come out to watch the Jarrow Crusade pass by.

Elizabeth is wearing a tailor-made suit with astrakhan for the collar, epaulettes and narrow edging at the wrists. Her hat has a turned up brim and is decorated with a feather and veil.

Robert is wearing a three-piece tailored suit, a snap brim hat and a striped tie.

1936 was also the year that King Edward VII abdicated in order to marry Mrs Wallis Simpson. Mrs Simpson loved to wear beautiful clothes and had many outfits by famous designers like Schiaparelli and Mainbocher. Because of the publicity surrounding her relationship with the King of England she was observed by women throughout the world, who copied her elegant looks and chic clothes. Find out more about her and draw pictures of her in some of her designer outfits.

A Shopping Expedition, c. 1937

Here are Emmeline and Elizabeth, who have met in London to go on a shopping expedition. They have just had afternoon tea in a smart restaurant. They are both wearing Schiaparelli suits.

With Europe drifting towards war, the line in women's clothes has become more masculine in appearance. The fashionable shape is for square, padded shoulders, slim hips and a tiny waist and for the first time in history women's shoulders are exaggerated to be larger than their hips. (This look is, in fact, very similar to the 1980s fashions worn in the popular American 'soaps'. Try comparing the two.)

Both women have shoulder-length hair which is loosely curled into the nape of the neck. Emmeline has on a high crowned hat and Elizabeth is wearing a flat 'coolie' style hat. They both wear black court shoes and gloves. The severity of the line of their suits is softened with decorative buttons, and Emmeline wears two cupid clips on her lapels. (Schiaparelli was renowned for her love of novelty buttons and clips.)

Also pictured here are some of Emmeline and Elizabeth's purchases. Emmeline bought a short fox fur coat for the winter and Elizabeth bought a sun dress as she and Robert are going on a short cruise. Along with several other dresses, shoes and jackets, the two women purchased hats and a few accessories like gloves, scarves and hair clips.

Draw pictures of some of the other things that they might have gone home with.

short silver fox coat

halter-neck sundress

summer hat with veil and flowers

hat with ribbon decoration

hair clips

59

Conclusion, 1939

It is now 1939 and Britain is at war with Germany. Charles is still working at his practice in Harley Street while Emmeline and the children have moved out of London and are staying at their country home for safety.

In order to help in the war effort Emmeline has decided to take in some evacuee children who have been sent to the country, away from the dangers of London. She is meeting them at the station.

She is wearing a knee-length day dress which is fitted over the bust, waist and hips and has padded shoulders and a belt at the waist. Over this she is wearing a loose coat with fitted shoulders and full sleeves which are gathered into the wrist. Her hat is decorated with artificial flowers and a veil.

The evacuee children are feeling very lost and bewildered. Although they are young they have had to leave their parents behind and come and live in a strange place with a strange family. They are all wearing their outdoor coats, socks and stout shoes. They have labels around their necks showing their names and addresses and they are carrying gas masks over their shoulders. Only one child has a case, the rest have their belongings in a pillow case.

How do you think it would have felt to be an evacuee child during the Second World War? What would it have been like to take in an evacuee child?

So now we come to the end of our period, which began with the freedom and euphoria of post-war Britain and ends with another war just beginning. We have seen the gaiety of the Bright Young Things and the despair of the unemployed, the beautiful designer clothes worn by the rich contrasted with the drab clothes of those with little money. The glamour of the Hollywood movie stars has brought fashion to a greater number of people and the availability of man-made fibres and mass produced clothes has meant that more women can now afford to be fashionable. During the course of your studies you might like to find out more about how technological advances like these affected the clothes people wore.

Finally, you could think about how a person's dress reflects his circumstances. Look at the drawings in this book and consider the context of the characters and ask yourself what their clothes are communicating about their lifestyle. What can you learn about a person just by looking at their clothes? Can you still guess a lot about someone today by looking at what they are wearing?

Glossary

astrakhan	The skin of young lambs from Astrakhan in Russia *(page 57)*
bar shoe	A shoe fastening with one or more straps over the instep *(pages 12, 14, 17, 21, 22, 29, 31, 37, 39, 45, 46, 47, 53)*
Byron bow	A large neck bow named after the poet Byron *(page 45)*
boudoir cap	A cap worn at night to protect the hair *(page 28)*
cami-knickers	All in one lady's undergarment (camisole and knickers) *(page 28)*
cloche hat	A bell-shaped hat with a deep crown and small or no brim *(pages 11, 13, 17)*
coatette	A lady's jumper-like garment often made of jersey or velveteen *(page 35)*
coolie hat	A lady's hat after the style of those worn by Chinese labourers *(page 59)*
epaulettes	Ornamental shoulder pieces *(page 57)*
jabot	A frill or ruffle worn at the neck to decorate the front of the bodice *(page 13)*
knickerbockers	A form of men's breeches which became popular for country and sporting wear *(page 9)*
lisle	A fine, twisted thread *(page 17)*
Louis heels	Heels with curved fronts *(page 18)*
lounge suit	A matching jacket and trousers suit, the jacket having a short skirt with rounded corners and a slightly fitted waist *(pages 8, 36, 43, 57)*
morocain	A silk or wool fabric with a crêpe weave *(page 10)*
organdie	A very fine transparent muslin *(page 31)*
Oxford bags	Wide legged men's trousers *(page 16)*
rayon	Artificial silk made from cellulose *(page 55)*
shingled hair	Cut very short at the back *(page 15, 18)*
snapbrim hat	A hat with a trilby shape, worn with the brim turned down at the front and up at the back *(page 36, 57)*
spats	Short gaiters covering the ankle made of canvas and buttoning under the foot *(page 8)*
tulle	Fine silk net used for veils and dresses *(page 18)*

Places to Visit

Here are a few ideas for some interesting places to visit connected with costume in the 1920s and 1930s.

Bath Museum of Costume, Assembly Rooms, Bath, Avon.

Gallery of English Costume, Platt Hall, Platt Fields, Rusholme, Manchester M14 5LL.

Museum of London, London Wall, London EC2Y 5HN.

Victoria and Albert Museum, Cromwell Road, South Kensington, London SW7 2RL.

Many small provincial museums have items of clothing from this period. Visit your local museum and ask them if they have any items of interest.

c. 1920

Book List

Black, J.A. & Garland, M.   *A history of fashion*, 2nd ed., Orbis Publishing, 1980
Bradfield, Nancy   *Costume in detail 1730-1930*, Harrap, 1968
Bradfield, Nancy   *Historical costumes of England 1066-1956*, Harrap, 1958
Braun-Ronsdorf, Margarete   *The Wheel of Fashion*, Thames & Hudson, 1964
Byrde, Penelope   *The Twentieth Century – Visual history of costume series*, Batsford, 1986
Carter, Ernestine   *The changing world of fashion*, Weidenfeld & Nicolson, 1977
Carter, Ernestine   *Twentieth century fashion*, Eyre Methuen, 1975
Contini, Mila   *Fashion – from ancient Egypt to the present day*, Hamlyn, 1965
Cookson, Catherine   *Catherine Cookson country*, Heinemann, 1986
Cunnington, C.W. & P.   *History of underclothes*, revised ed., Faber, 1981
Cunnington, P. & Mansfield, A.   *Handbook of English costume in the Twentieth century*, Faber, 1973
DeMarly, Diana   *Working Dress*, Batsford, 1986
Dorner, Jane   *Fashion*, Octopus books, 1974
Dorner, Jane   *Fashion in the twenties and thirties*, Ian Allan, 1973
Sunderland Echo   *Canny aad Sunlun . . .* Portsmouth & Sunderland Newspapers plc., 1983
Ewing, E.   *Dress and Undress*, Batsford, 1978
Ewing, E.   *History of children's costume*, Batsford, 1977
Foster, Vanda   *Bags and purses*, Batsford, 1982
Gaisford, John (Ed.)   *Times gone by – a photographic record of Britain 1856-1956*, Marshall Cavendish, 1985
Hall, Carolyn   *The thirties in Vogue*, Octopus, 1984
Howell, Georgina   *In Vogue – six decades of fashion*, Allen Lane, 1975
Laver, James   *Costume and fashion, a concise history*, 2nd ed. Thames & Hudson, 1982
Laver, James   *Costume through the ages*, Thames & Hudson, 1964
Laver, James   *Taste and fashion*, 2nd ed., Harrap, 1945
Packer, William   *The art of Vogue covers 1909-1940*, Octopus, 1981
Pagnamenta, P. & Overy, R.   *All our working lives*, B.B.C., 1984
Purkiss, Sallie etc.   *Home, the town and work in the 1930s*, Longman, 1983
Victoria and Albert Museum   *400 years of fashion*, 1984
White, Palmer   *Elsa Schiaparelli*, Aurum Press, 1986
Whiteman, Von   *Looking at fashion 1901-1939*, E.P. Publishing, 1978
Wood, Sydney   *The thirties*, Oliver and Boyd, 1984

c. 1922

Things to Do

1. Talk to any of your relatives who were alive in the 1920s and 1930s. Ask them about the clothes that they used to wear. Do they have any photographs? Do they have any old clothes in their attic?

2. Find out all you can about make-up and hairstyles in the 1920s and 1930s. How were they influenced by Hollywood? Find out more about some of the famous filmstars like Joan Crawford, Marlene Dietrich and Shirley Temple. How did they influence fashion?

3. Find out about the beauty business. What kind of electrical gadgets were used for curling hair, perming hair and massage?

4. Look at some of the technical developments that took place in the manufacture of fabrics during this period. Find out about elastic, rayon and nylon.

5. Have a look at the sports clothes worn by men and women of the 1920s and 1930s. How are they different from those worn today? Draw pictures of some of the garments.

6. Find out about some of the chain stores that were becoming popular during the 1920s and 1930s. Write to a large chain store like Marks and Spencer and ask them what kind of clothes they were selling at that time.

7. Look back at the story of John. Imagine more of the people that he might have met on his journey from the north to the south of England. Draw pictures of some of these people.

8. Find out about the dance craze in the 1920s. Draw pictures of the clothes that people wore in the dance halls.

9. Imagine a rich couple going on a cruise on a huge liner. Draw pictures of some of the other passengers in their fashionable clothes and also of some of the many men and women who work on board the ship. For example, cooks, waiters, cleaners, the dance band etc.

c. 1929